Learning Journeys with ICT

Early Years

Angie Simmons

essential
resources

Title: Learning Journeys with ICT
Early Years

Author: Angie Simmons

Designer: Delineate Ltd

Editor: Tanya Tremewan

Book code: 230G

ISBN: 978-1-877523-08-3

Published: 2009

Publisher: Essential Resources Educational Publishers Limited

United Kingdom:	**Australia:**	**New Zealand:**
Unit 8–10 Parkside	PO Box 90	PO Box 5036
Shortgate Lane	Oak Flats	Invercargill
Laughton, BN8 6DG	NSW 2529	
ph: 0845 3636 147	ph: 1800 005 068	ph: 0800 087 376
fax: 0845 3636 148	fax: 1800 981 213	fax: 0800 937 825

Website: www.essentialresourcesuk.com

About the author: Angie Simmons is an ICT adviser and educator. She enjoys working with teachers as they learn to use ICT as a tool to enhance learning. She is interested in current best-practice learning approaches that encompass thinking skills, collaboration and problem solving. Angie lives by the beach near Auckland, New Zealand with her husband, two border collies, a parrot and three cats. She is also an avid patchwork quilter and member of a local patchwork quilting club.

Contents

Introduction

Education in the early years, when most learning occurs, lays the foundation for all future learning. It is therefore paramount that, as educators, we set up learning experiences that will enable young children to meet the government objectives encapsulated in the Every Child Matters campaign for all children to:

- be healthy
- stay safe
- enjoy and achieve
- make a positive contribution
- experience economic wellbeing.

Providing effective learning situations to facilitate the optimum level of learning in the early years is what this book in the *Learning Journeys with ICT* series is all about. It shows some of the many positive ways to integrate ICT tools – both hardware and software – into teaching and learning in the early years. It also includes two case studies about the successful experiences of some of those who have done it already.

What is an effective learning situation?

Research has shown us that effective learning occurs when:

1. the teacher gives constructive feedback to guide and scaffold the learner
2. the learner is actively involved in the process
3. the learner is made aware of the relevance of and connections to prior learning and of the big picture of learning a new concept
4. the learner is in a safe and positive environment
5. the learning experience allows for socially mediated learning.

This research on best learning and teaching practice fits well with a social constructivist framework, which recognises the social nature of acquiring language and literacies.

The findings on the research on effective learning are embedded in the principles of the Early Years Foundation Stage curriculum. Its principles under the Learning and Development theme emphasise the child's active involvement in the learning process and the value of learning through experience and alongside others. The Enabling Environments theme covers all aspects of the learning environment that need to be taken into consideration in facilitating children's learning.

The Foundation Stage curriculum has been developed concurrently with the Primary Framework for Literacy and Mathematics, and makes many links to it. This alignment means that the transition to school from early childhood education is as seamless as possible and builds on the child's experiences, while affirming their identity.

The role of ICT in effective learning

So how can information and communication technology (ICT) tools scaffold the process of learning within the parameters for effective learning? We need to look at how the teacher can create learning situations, using ICT tools, where the child has a safe and supported learning experience and can actively take part in exploring concepts in their world.

*ICT tools need to be used **by** children.*

We also need to move from using ICT as an administrative tool to using it as a tool for learning. ICT tools need to be used **by** the children. After all, the preschoolers of today will be the users of technologies we have not yet dreamed of. ICT is already an integral part of their world now and its role will only grow in their future.

Over the last few years, early learning institutions have been utilising computers for administration purposes and for children to use with suitable software. Digital cameras are now widely used for recording children's learning experiences. Recently some educators have also been using data projectors, widescreen television sets and interactive whiteboards to share the learning with a wider audience.

Some argue that children should not be introduced to ICT tools at such an early age on the grounds that they should be actively exploring their environment and learning through their involvement in the world around them. I agree with this emphasis on active exploration and hands-on learning. At the same time, integrating ICT tools into the teaching and learning programme can actually assist child's exploration of their world: if these tools are integrated well, young children do not just sit passively at a computer by themselves, being led by the software application. Further, as we live in a society that is increasingly bound up with ICT, it makes sense to make these tools part of education so that children are seamlessly integrating them into their lives in both home and formal learning environments.

The pedagogy behind the process

What is important when we use ICT tools in the early childhood setting is to firmly embed them within the context of best practice teaching and learning. ICT tools should be used to enhance the curriculum so that they support the child's learning.

Given what we know about the key characteristics of an effective learning situation (see above), we need to situate learning with ICT tools within the context of the active and social learner. The table on the next page shows how the roles of teacher and learner have developed as the pedagogy has changed. As it demonstrates, we need to look for ICT tools to support and scaffold the learner in the knowledge-building process, as we take a social constructivist approach to learning.

ICT tools need to be situated within the context of the active and social learner.

These children are learning in a socially mediated context – learning from and with each other.

How a pedagogy affects the use of ICT in teaching and learning

Pedagogy	Child's role	Teacher's role	Outcome	Relevant ICT tool(s)
Information transfer	Passive – listens and receives information	Provides knowledge	The child may or may not attend to the information and may not develop a real understanding of the information given.	Computer application that the child has no interaction with, such as Encarta
Behaviourism	Responds to stimulus	Sets up situations where children make correct responses to stimuli; feedback is directed at the right/wrong response	Rote learning takes place and the child often does not have a deep understanding of the concept or process.	Drill-and-practice programs that just require a response, such as Reader Rabbit
Constructivism	Active participant – builds on prior knowledge; actively involved in the feedback process	Facilitates the learning so children can experience and make connections; seeks feedback from children and guides them with constructive feedback	Child learns more effectively through being actively involved in the learning process.	Open-ended programs that can be controlled by the user, such as Word, KidPix, PowerPoint or iPhoto Digital camera Interactive whiteboard
Social constructivism	Active participant with others	Facilitates the learning so children can experience learning situations with others in a socially mediated situation	The child learns through interaction with the environment and peers, and builds new knowledge that is related to their own schemata or ideas.	All ICT tools as mentioned with constructivism above, but used collaboratively with children grouped around the ICT tools and working together to interact with the ICT tools and discuss ideas

A. ICT tools for the early years

The following ICT tools are among those that are most suitable for the early years. They have been selected as they cover not only the "I" for information processing in ICT but also the all-important "C" for communication. The hardware covered in this section is:

- digital still camera
- digital video camera
- digital blue camera
- listening post
- computer
- data projector
- interactive whiteboard.

Along with some ideas for using each of these tools, this section mentions software and accessories that are helpful or necessary in operating them. Section B then deals with the "how to" of using some of the software in more detail.

Other ICT hardware not listed here, but which you may find useful in the early childhood setting, includes the fax, robotic tools, whiteboard and mimio, shared headsets, palm pilot, and tablet PC.

Digital still camera

The digital camera is one of the most useful ICT tools for the early years in education. It is preferable to an analogue camera as you and the children can:

- see the photo immediately after it has been taken
- delete an image and start again if needed
- use the digital images in a variety of ways when downloaded from the camera.

Digital photos of children's learning experiences can be used for reflective analysis for both children and teachers. This approach provides assessment for learning through the medium of **learning stories**. These learning stories can be shared with the child's family, who may also contribute to the learning story portfolio for their child by adding their own stories from home. (See Section B for more on this highly successful way of putting ICT tools to work.)

Choosing a digital still camera

You may find the following pointers useful when choosing from the wide selection of digital cameras that is available:

- The digital camera should be robust and easy to use.
- It should have recognisable icons for various functions, such as arrows to show direction when viewing.
- A large screen to play back the photos for review is useful.
- If a camera has a video recording component, check that the button to take videos is well away from the button to take still photos. If choosing a camera with a video function, bear in mind that videos take up a lot of space on the memory card.
- Check whether the battery is included in the price and, if it is not, how much a battery costs.

After buying your camera, read the instruction booklet carefully so you can create the settings that will be most useful for your purposes.

Software and accessories

Most digital cameras have the capacity to insert a **memory card**, which stores your photos. The memory card is not usually included in the price of the camera and its price varies according to the amount of memory it has.

The digital camera also comes with **software to download the photos** from the camera. If you have a Mac, or a PC with a recent version of Windows, the platform generally recognises any digital camera. (With older versions of Windows, you need to load the software onto your computer.) When the camera is connected to a Mac, the iPhoto application immediately appears and all you need to do is click on the Import button.

A **card reader** is handy when you want to download your photos quickly on any computer as it enables you to use memory cards from a variety of cameras without downloading each camera's software. You can insert the memory card into the card reader and then insert the cable into the computer to retrieve photos from the memory card.

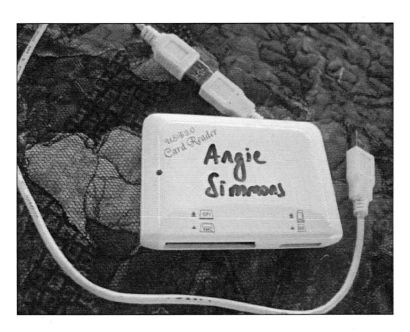

A card reader: insert the memory card from the camera in the appropriate slot for the size of the memory card, then plug the cable into the computer to download your photos. A pop-up menu will appear guiding you through this process.

Ideas for using the digital still camera

- Go on a shape walk with the camera, during which the children find shapes in the environment and take pictures of them. You can put the photos into a slide show using iPhoto or PowerPoint and use them for discussion and learning.

- Children take photos of each other with different expressions. Use the photos to discuss emotions and feelings. Put them into an electronic or printed book with repetitive text, such as *I feel sad when … I feel happy when … I feel angry when …* When children relate their experiences, write them as captions to go in the book. Children love to read their own personalised books and will revisit them again and again.

- Use the child's own native language (perhaps bringing in family members to help) to create personal stories to go with their photos of activities around the centre or class. In this way, you recognise and nurture diversity, including different cultural values, and have a personal story to send home for sharing with family and friends.

- Take the digital camera on trips or use it to record special events. Create a slide show using KidPix or PowerPoint and show it to the children, preferably with a data projector (or large screen TV display) connected to the computer. Encourage them to look carefully at the photos and use describing words about the photos, which you record on the computer so they can see the words appear on the screen and "read" them. If you do not have this technology, have the same discussion with a small group of children sitting around the computer with you.

- Take photos to record a sequence of events for a "how to" poster. For example, you could use the photos of a cooking session to display the steps in creating the recipe.

- Take mystery photos (by zooming in on objects) and make them into a "What am I?" slide show using PowerPoint. Add clues using the custom animation feature for the children to make guesses; the final animation reveals the answer. As an alternative to creating a slide show, print them out and use them for discussion time on the mat.

- Use photos taken in the centre or class to create jigsaw puzzles. Divide up each jigsaw with Word or PowerPoint drawing tools (see the information on desktop publishing in Section B) and insert the parts into an electronic slide show. As a manual alternative, enlarge the photo and print it, cut it into sections and laminate it.

- Show the children how to use the Image toolbar in Picture Manager or another photo editing program on the computer. They change their photos using the various effects available.

- Insert photos in Paint or KidPix and add extras with the paintbrush or text tool. Make a special frame around photos or add pirate masks to images of the children.

- With the macro function of the camera, take close-up photos of insects and use the photos to discuss the features of each insect.

- Go for a walk on which you take photos of road signs. Discuss features of road signs with reference to the photos before the children design and create their own road sign.

- Take the children on a walk to look at buildings in the community. Take photos to feature later in a discussion on the design and features of buildings.

Digital video camera

A digital video camera is a useful tool for reflection and analysis. It is also handy for recording important events or learning experiences to share with children, parents and staff.

Choosing a digital video camera

There are a variety of options to decide among when buying a video camera. Choose one that has:

- simple and recognisable instructions
- the basic functions rather than a whole range of optional extras as well.

Ideally, your school or centre would have two video cameras: one for staff to record events or children's learning experiences, and one that children can use for their own learning.

Pointers for using a digital video camera

The camera illustrated below was purchased in the United States for $299, and is simple and easy to use. The settings of other models may vary somewhat but the basic principles remain fairly constant. Where this camera uses a tape, some newer cameras have inbuilt hard drives. On the down side, they are a lot more expensive and more can go wrong with them.

*With the camera in **VCR mode** you can play the tape back or find places on the tape with the fast forward or backwards buttons.*

Connect your cables to the camera or computer here. The screen on this camera swivels around so you can view from any angle.

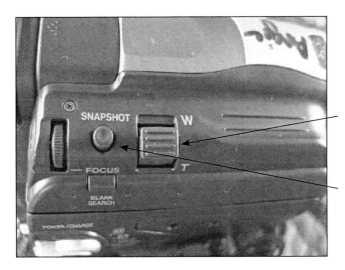

The sliding button here allows you to zoom in or out of your focus area.

You can take still shots with the snapshot button.

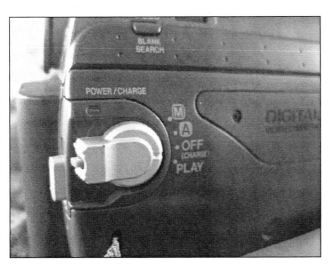

*When the camera is in play mode you can view your footage. **A** stands for Automatic – use this setting to record your video. Turn your camera off after taking any footage to save the battery power.*

Working with your video footage

To download footage from the camera:

- start up your computer's video editing program
- connect the cable between the computer's USB port and the camera
- turn the camera on to play mode
- get your video to start downloading in clips by:
  - on the Mac, clicking on the import button that appears after you have clicked on the camera icon under the viewing screen
  - on the PC, opening Movie Maker and clicking "Import video" on the side menu bar.

To reduce the file size you have to import, do an initial edit of your footage on the camera first.

For more refined editing on the computer, you need the relevant software. Although a range of video editing applications is available, editing can be very time consuming and it usually is most effective if you keep to well-known and simple applications such as:

- Movie Maker 2, which comes as a Windows accessory on the PC
- iMovie, which is part of the iLife suite of programs that comes with the Mac.

For ideas on using the video camera in the early years, see the end of the next subsection on the digital blue camera.

In preparation for downloading your footage, connect the camera by cable to the USB port of your computer.

Import your footage into your computer using your movie editing program.

Digital Blue (still and video) camera

The Digital Blue camera takes very short videos (up to four minutes) and snapshots. If you have an external microphone, it can also be used as a web camera to record your voice and image when it is plugged into the computer (PC only).

This camera is a useful investment for teaching and learning in the early years because it is:

- well suited for use by young children – robust, simple and with user friendly controls
- reasonably priced.

Children hold the centre stalk to bring the eyepiece up to their eye and point the Digital Blue camera. To capture their chosen image, they either click the snapshot button or press the video icon. The camera is made of durable plastic.

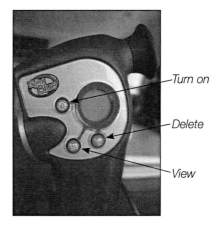

Turn on

Delete

View

The Digital Blue camera is made of plastic and is robust.

Importing your film from the camera and editing your shots

1. Place the camera in the dock and connect the cable between the computer's USB port and camera (with the camera turned on).

2. Open the Digital Blue software program and click on the camera icon. Tick the option that pops up asking if you want to download the items on the camera. Your video and still shots will go into the temporary items view of the image library; a message will ask if you want to put the items into the permanent library and you can choose the items you wish to store there (see screenshot on the next page).

This is the first screenshot to appear when you open your Digital Blue software program. Click on the camera to begin. The scissors represent the editing mode when you are editing the photos and videos from your library of imported shots.

Note: To import any photos or video (avi format) files from your computer, click on the import button, which brings up your computer menu. You can then track back to find the photos or videos you wish to import into your software library.

3. To add your photos to the timeline clip viewer (where you will edit your shots), click Add or drag and drop them there.

In the image library, you select photos from the temporary items view to add to the permanent library, which already contains standard items that are available for you to use as backgrounds. Click the arrow on the right to close the library when you have finished placing all your shots on the timeline.

4. Edit your shots, using three main tools on the right hand side of the screen: text editing, special video effects and sound effects (see screenshots that follow).

5. Click on the icon of hands to prepare to share your production via a viewing screen, screen saver or printed hard copy. Although it is possible to export your video as a wmv or jpg file from the collections library, the sound files will not be exported so, to share your video, you really need to do it in the digital blue software.

Note: Use the help menu to find out more.

Select the text editing tool by clicking on the first of three main buttons on the right.

Here, the text editing tool is being used to overlay text on the selected video clip or photo. A range of options for formatting the text is available. Click away from the text to make the white around the text disappear so that the text is floating over the shot.

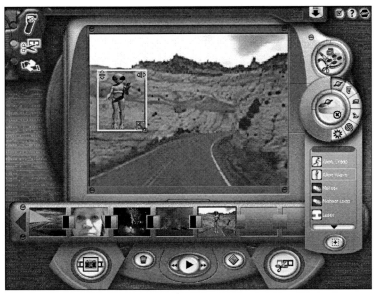

The middle button on the right gives you access to a wide range of special video effects. Overlay the video clip or photo with characters or various other animated objects.

The bottom button on the right allows you to bring in your own sound files (wav files only). Alternatively, you can make use of the great range of special effects sounds and music files available in the program.

Go to the viewing screen area for sharing with other viewers.

Make a screensaver.

Print your production.

Click on the hands icon in the top lefthand corner to get this screen, where you can prepare to share your production.

Ideas for using the digital video camera

- Film children's learning experiences and display them during mat times so they can revisit and discuss the learning. When viewed as a whole, the learning experience becomes more meaningful. Moreover, by discussing it together, the children will be engaging in reflective practice and socially mediated learning.

- Film children's performances and put them on a CD or DVD for taking home to share with family and friends. Film practice sessions for children to review and see where they need to make improvements to their performance.

- Film trips and events for children to view and experience again.

- With the children, discuss and plan role plays and stories, in which toys and other props will feature. Encourage them to film their own productions.

- Go on a nature walk, using the zoom function of the camera to see right inside flowers and close-ups of insects and spiders down in the grass.

- Use the camera to develop a theme such as insects. Film the children making insect shapes using their bodies or objects, moving like insects, singing insect songs and zooming in on real insects. Put all the segments of film together to create a special video about the topic. Although it may take some time for you to put together, this kind of activity has the advantages of involving all the children in creating and filming, and becoming a permanent record that can be stored and viewed again and again.

- Make a numbers video, in which the children create number sentences with their bodies or objects, sing number songs and use different languages for numbers. You and the children can film it and put it together as a personalised learning video for your centre or class.

Listening post

Children plug microphones into a central listening post device, which links to an audio recorder. They can listen to recorded stories as they turn the pages in a book.

Children can follow along with a recorded story at a listening post.

Computer

As well as being useful for running ICT activities itself, the computer is a useful supporting tool for other hardware (eg, to download photos and footage from digital cameras).

Choosing a computer and supporting equipment

When choosing a computer and associated equipment for young children, you need to consider:

- the option of a laptop, given that it can be moved easily and used anywhere
- the advantages of a desk top, such as that it is robust and, because it has a separate keyboard and monitor, the whole system is not affected if something goes wrong
- whether to choose a Mac or PC as your operating platform
- effective antivirus software, which should be installed on all computers
- effective filtering software, such as Watchdog or Net Nanny so that children are not exposed to the dangers of using the Internet without restrictions
- suitable seating so that the children can look at the computer at face level with their feet touching the ground
- a mouse with a design that makes it easier for young children to use
- a keyboard with a design especially suitable for young children.

With regard to the decision on whether to use a PC or a Mac, your choice may be partly influenced by the software each platform supports. Although most applications run on both, there are some differences between them.

The **Mac** has:

- an inbuilt microphone, which is useful for recording children's voices
- an inbuilt web camera and the Photo Booth program (in newer models), which the children love to use to turn photos of themselves into strange people
- integrated media applications that link together to create slide shows, e-books, calendars, videos and other integrated media, and that come with the Mac as part of your computer purchase. The applications are: iPhoto, for image editing and storage; iMovie, for editing video and still photos to create films; iTunes, for storage of audio recordings; and GarageBand, for creating, recording or editing audio (sound).

The Mac also runs the standard Windows Office suite of programs and runs most software programs such as KidPix, Kidspiration and the various CD-ROM activities applications.

The **PC** supports various kinds of software, including:

- the standard Windows Office applications
- a range of accessories such as Movie Maker, Picture Manager (or Photo Editor for earlier versions) and Paint.

You need an external microphone to record on older PC models.

Children work collaboratively on PCs.
Note the headphones.

Ideas for using the computer

- Take photos of the children, download the photos onto the computer and use Word to create speech bubbles beginning "Hi, I am ..." so that one comes out of the mouth of each child. (For instructions on how, see the information on desktop publishing in Section B.) Each child keys in their name in the speech bubble linked to their photo. Print out the photos and place them on the wall as a class portrait gallery.

18

Interactive whiteboard

Although it can be an expensive item, the interactive whiteboard is a wonderful learning tool for the early years as it offers great kinaesthetic learning opportunities. A data projector linked to a computer displays the computer screen on the interactive whiteboard. Then children can interact directly with the large whiteboard screen, performing all the functions of a mouse directly on the board with either their fingers or a special pen. They can, for example, move items, change their handwritten letters to type at the touch of a button, move objects and letters around on the screen and undertake a variety of learning activities that are part of the software that comes with the interactive whiteboard.

The two main types of interactive whiteboard are:

1. the Promethean Activboard, which has a durable hard screen and requires special pens for writing on it
2. the SMART Board, which has a membrane surface that allows the user to write on the screen with their finger.

Children work on the interactive whiteboard to learn spelling. They are using the special pen tools and writing with their fingers.

A similar but cheaper tool is the Mimio board. This apparatus connects to a normal whiteboard and relays the image from the computer screen to project it on the whiteboard. When you can write on this normal whiteboard, the interface of the Mimio board technology saves it to your computer.

Ideas for using the interactive whiteboard

- In a Word document, insert photos of the children into an AutoShape. (For instructions on how, see the information on desktop publishing in Section B.) Place these photos to one side of the document and create a large, empty circle (using the circle drawing tool) on the other side. When children arrive, they drag their photo inside the circle – so that it becomes a visual attendance register.
- Children use the magic pen tools to practise writing their names.
- Make a cache of favourite interactive website games in Bookmarks or Favorites in your web browser, so children can get together in groups to play them on the big screen.

- Run educational interactive programs displayed on the interactive whiteboard. For example, with Sunshine Galaxy Maths, children move objects (eg, put butterflies in a jar) and count them.

- Run ArtRage or KidPix displayed on the interactive whiteboard. Children make virtual paintings with their fingers (SMART Board) or special pen tools (Activboard).

- Use the interactive games and activities that come with the whiteboard, such as the clock and the Flash animation games and activities.

- Use the shape tools to set up random shapes on the screen. Children move the shapes around to make pictures.

- Use Google educator tools with the interactive capabilities of the interactive whiteboard. Students can explore environments beyond the classroom walls, and annotate and save relevant images and movies for learning experiences and reflection or group work. Great tools include:

  - Google Earth, which includes both virtual trips all over the world and video tutorials about the universe

  - Google Moon, with authentic footage of the Apollo landings

  - Google Mars, which offers detailed, interactive maps of Mars

  - Google Sky, with interactive maps of the galaxies

  - Google SketchUp, a free application with which students can create and explore 3D sketches. It interacts with other Google applications and works well as an activity on the interactive whiteboard as students can create their 3D sketch and manipulate it directly.

Working on the interactive whiteboard, students make 3D sketches in Google SketchUp, then place them in the Google Earth environment or in the 3D Warehouse environment to interact with other 3D dimensions.

 To access these great resources for the interactive whiteboard, go to Google for Educators (www.google.com/educators).

Tip: For more information on how to use this versatile tool, see another book in this series, *Learning Journeys with ICT: Interactive Whiteboards.*

B. Putting software to use

A wide range of software lends itself well to teaching and learning in the early years. This section outlines applications you can use to:

- produce creative stories and poems
- work with graphics (creating and editing images)
- make videos and slide shows
- create your own radio show by podcasting
- do desktop publishing
- create learning stories.

Producing creative stories and poems

Kidspiration (story writing with pictures)

Kidspiration is a mindmapping software program that is picture based. You can add libraries of other images such as children's photos, along with graphics that the children have created using the program's paint tools.

You and the children can use Kidspiration in the following ways:

- Create brainstorms about a topic.
- Build a mindmap using pictures and then click on the writing view to turn it into a written story.
- Use the SuperGrouper function to classify objects. For instance, make the shopping trolley into a SuperGrouper picture (so that you can drag objects into it) and the children find pictures of healthy foods to drag into the trolley. Use the heart to drag all their favourite activities into the heart.
- Use the painting tool for the children to create their own portraits. Store the portraits in the picture library, to make a class library, and then children can drag their selected portrait on the screen in the same way as all the other pictures.
- Insert photos from a class trip into the picture library. Use them to make stories or mindmaps about the trip.

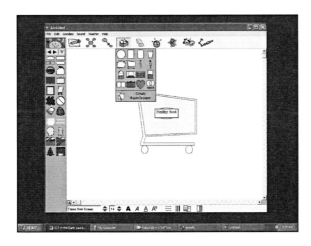

By selecting a picture under the SuperGrouper icon, you create a picture into which children can drag and drop objects. For example, children can find the healthy food shown in the library of food objects and drag and drop it into the SuperGrouper shopping trolley.

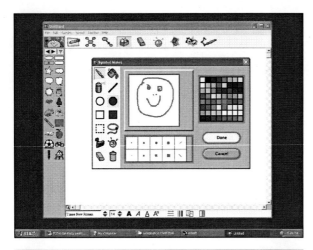

This paint option is activated by the paintbrush icon on the far right of the top menu bar. Children can use it to paint their own picture and save it for the Kidspiration library.

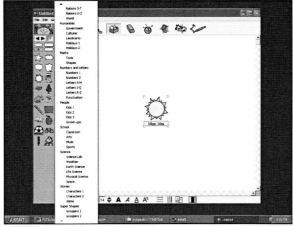

If you click on the arrow at the side of the picture library, you can see all the categories of pictures there. Drag a picture from the side to start the mindmap and, while small highlighting squares are surrounding it, you can click on the bubble map in the top menu bar to add a bubble. Change it into another picture by clicking on the picture of your choice while the bubble is selected.

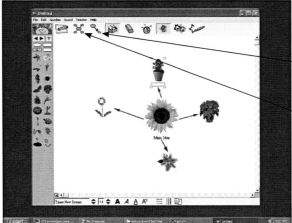

Icon for making another link

Picture view icon to create mindmaps

A mindmap shows related objects that you have dragged from the picture library in the picture view.

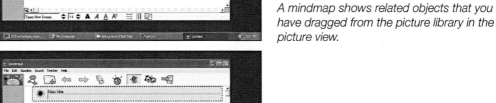

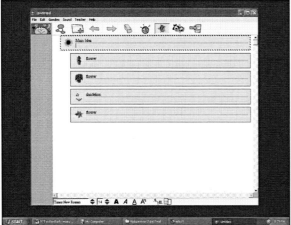

In writing view, children can write their story or dictate it to the teacher.

24

Max's Toolbox (PC)

Max's Toolbox works in conjunction with the Microsoft Office suite of programs. All the programs are equivalent to the Microsoft Office versions – such as Word, PowerPoint and Excel. What is different is that the Max's Toolbox programs have pictorial icons, so that learning to use them is far easier for young children.

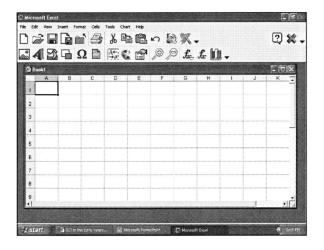

MaxCount is a pictorial version of Excel.

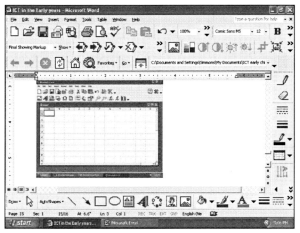

MaxWrite is a pictorial version of Word.

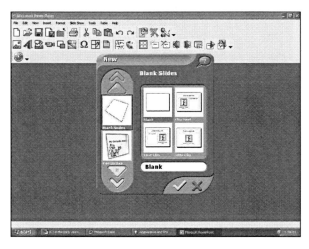

MaxShow is a pictorial version of PowerPoint.

Working with graphics

Picture Manager 💿

Picture Manager is part of the Windows XP package. If you have an earlier PC, you may have Photo Editor, which works in much the same way.

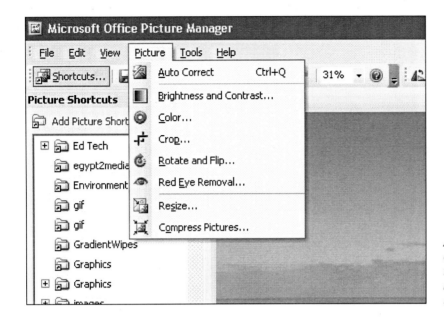

A range of editing options is available from the Picture menu in the top menu bar of Picture Manager.

Follow these steps to edit your photos in Picture Manager.

1. Be sure you have saved all the pictures you will need in the My Pictures folder.

2. Locate Picture Manager, which is under Tools in the Microsoft Office folder (accessed by going to All Programs in the Start menu).

3. Double click on the picture you want to edit.

4. Choose Picture in the top menu bar to choose what you need to do to your picture:

   • Use Auto Correct to adjust the picture to a better quality automatically.

   • As an alternative to Auto Correct, adjust the brightness and contrast yourself (eg, if you have a dark or dull picture or if there is too much light). Select the Brightness and Contrast option, then move the slider at the side to make your adjustments.

   • Use Color to adjust the colour.

   • To cut off some of the picture, choose the Crop option, which will create handles on the side of the picture (see screenshot on the next page). Pick up each handle in turn and drag it with the move tool (the cross that appears as you hover) until the handles are surrounding the part of the picture you want to keep and then click OK. Alternatively, use the adjustments in the side menu. To keep your original, uncropped picture, use Save As to save the cropped picture with a different name (eg, "lion ear" instead of "lion").

   • With Red Eye Removal, you can remove the red from people's eyes that sometimes appears in photos taken with a flash.

   • To resize, choose the Resize option, grab one of the handles that appear on the corners of the picture and drag till the picture is the size you need.

- Use Compress Pictures to reduce your picture's file size (ie, the amount of memory needed to store it), which can be useful if you are sending it by email or putting it on the web. As data are lost when you compress a picture, keep the original, good quality one and use Save As to save the compressed one with a different name (eg, with "web" after the original name).

Note: To compress all the pictures in a Word file at the same time (eg, in a newsletter that you are emailing out or posting on the web), use the Compress Pictures command, which is in the Picture toolbar.

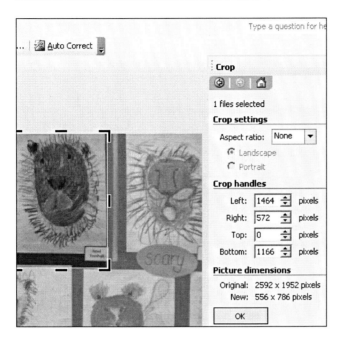

To position the crop handles around the part of the picture you want to keep, click on each handle in turn and drag it with the move tool to the place you want, then click OK. Save your cropped picture with a different name so you keep the original.

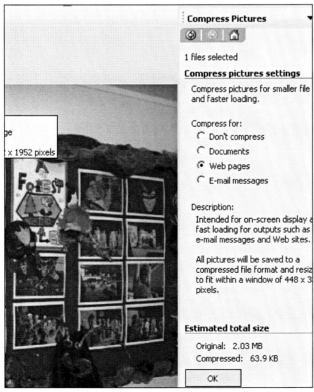

When you compress your graphic (make it a smaller file size), you select the purpose for which you are compressing it. For example, here the graphic will be uploaded onto the web.

iPhoto

iPhoto is the image editing program that comes bundled with the Mac. From its photo library, where all the photos are stored, you can create your own album (folder) and turn it into an e-book, card, calendar or slide show that includes music.

Create albums for your photos to make it easy to retrieve them, and to create themed slide shows and e-books.

Double click on a photo to open it up in the Edit menu. Click on the double arrow on the right to open the Effects or Adjust menu.

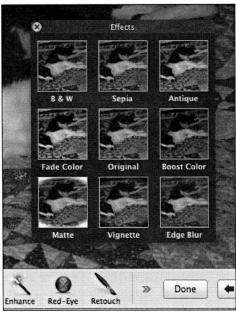

Under the Effects menu, you can decide on the "look" of your photo.

It is easy to edit your photos using the range of options available from the editing tools, including:

- a range of effects (eg, sepia, matt, edge blur) under the Effects menu

- a range of size options (including custom sizing that you set yourself) under the Constrain menu

- picture adjustments (see screenshot below) under the Adjust menu.

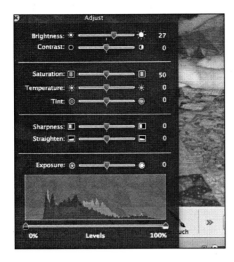

Using the options under the Adjust menu can make a big difference to your photo. Make those dark corners bright by moving the sliders along.

Paint ⓟⓒ

Paint is the free imaging tool that comes with Windows software. It is located in the Accessories menu (accessed under All Programs in the Start menu). It is useful for:

- drawing pictures on screen
- embellishing photos or other graphics, such as with a background and caption.

Click on a colour from the range available at the bottom of the screen, select a pencil or paint brush tool from the icons on the left, and draw a picture in the Paint work area.

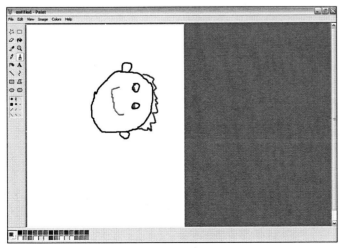

It is possible to manipulate the graphic in basic ways, such as rotation.

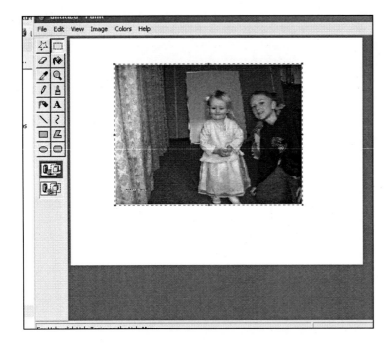

To bring a photo or another graphic into Paint, click on the select tool and drag the tool across the screen to create an area for your graphic. Under File in the top menu bar, go to Open and select the graphic you wish to appear in that area. To change the size of the selected picture, hover over the small blue points until you see an arrow and click and drag until the picture is the right size.

Fill bucket

Spray can

Text tool

Create a background with the fill bucket and overlay a decorative colour with the spray can. Use the text tool to write a caption or labels for your graphic.

Graphics created in Paint can also be imported into a Word document, for example, to illustrate a story you have written with the children.

ArtRage

ArtRage is a program with which children can create virtual paintings using a range of paint tools.

The starter edition of ArtRage is available free over the Internet. An upgraded version with extra tools is available at a cost. It includes a transparency option so children can insert a picture and put a virtual tracing paper over it then paint on this to copy it.

With ArtRage, children can create virtual paintings.

 Download the starter edition of ArtRage for free at Ambient Design's website (www.ambientdesign.com).

Publisher

Use Publisher to create your own professional brochures, newsletters, greeting cards and many more desktop publishing products.

To create wonderful greeting cards:

- ask children to draw pictures in Paint or KidPix (see more on KidPix in the next section, "Making videos and slide shows")
- save each picture as a gif file
- insert the picture into a greeting card in Publisher
- add the name of the illustrator and the organisation on the back of the card, if you choose
- print out the card, which is easy to fold into a professional-looking product to send home or use as a fundraiser.

For more on desktop publishing, see the information later in this section.

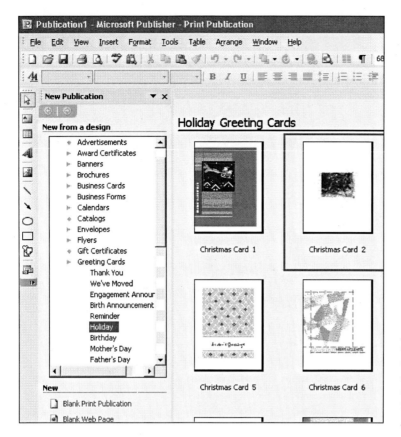

When you choose a theme, your card will pop up in an editing mode. The numbers at the bottom of the screen show each page that makes up the card. You can delete the existing images and insert your own.

Making videos and slide shows

KidPix Mac PC

This work was created by children using KidPix in the Maori immersion unit at Newton Central School, Auckland, New Zealand.

KidPix is a versatile program that can be put to use in a variety of ways in the early years. The following ideas are just a sampling:

- Create animated slide shows. For example, draw a seed in the ground, save the picture and open it again, then add another part of the growing sequence (eg, a shoot sprouting) and save this picture with another name. Continue adding growth features in this way, creating each new picture with the just-completed picture as a template but saving the new one with another name. Make your collection of pictures into a slide show with very fast timing so that, when you play the slide show, it looks like the plant is growing.

- Make beautiful frames around photos by using the stamp tool to surround the photo with small pictures, or by using the colourful pattern fill bucket to cover the screen and then the magic rubber to rub out the middle, then insert your photo to fit in the space.

- Children use the paintbrush or the animated alphabet in the animation section to practise writing their name.

- Using the text tool, children create text over photos and make a slide show for others to read as an electronic book. Where a child has a non English-speaking background, this tool is especially good for creating electronic storybooks in the child's own language.

This page has a photo as a background graphic, over which the student has added text and images and has painted the hills.

To make a slide show:

- create all the slides (pictures) you need – eg, from the Add menu in the top menu bar, you can select Add Graphic or Import Background
- switch to the slide show view
- click the red arrow to select the slides you wish to include
- click on the film camera arrow to activate the transition arrows
- click on a transition arrow to choose your transition and sound for each move from one slide to the next
- play the slide show and save it
- export the slide show (from the File menu in the top menu bar) to another format such as QuickTime Movie (mov) if you wish to share it in different ways, such as linking to other multimedia presentation tools.

In slide show view, you activate the Load Picture command by clicking the red arrow. From here you can choose the pictures to put in the slide show.

When you click on a transition arrow, you can choose the visual effect and sound that accompanies the change from one slide to the next.

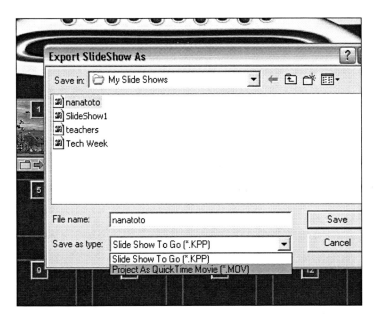

To save your slide show in a different format, such as QuickTime Movie, use the Export command in the File menu.

Photo Story 3

Photo Story 3 allows you to create an audiovisual digital story with your photos. In effect, it is an application for making photo movies.

Photo Story 3 is a free download for Windows XP users from the Microsoft website (www.microsoft.com). If you need to download Windows Media Player 10 and Direct X as well, you will be prompted to do so and these downloads will also be provided.

Follow these steps to create your photo movie:

- Open Photo Story 3, which is stored under All Programs in the Start menu and choose New Story from the pop-up menu that appears.

- Click Next to get a pop-up menu asking you to import photos. Select the photos that you wish to include from your computer files and they will appear at the bottom of the screen. (Note: To import all the photos in a folder at once, select them all by clicking the first file name and then holding the Ctrl key and letter A, and then import them all together.)

- Click Next for the text menu, which allows you to add text to each picture. (Note: This tool provides you with the basics. If you want any fancy pages – eg, for the title page – you can create them with images and WordArt in PowerPoint, save them in jpeg format and include them with your folder of photos for the photo movie.)

- Click Next to record narration for each photo. If you have an older PC model, you will need to plug in a microphone for this step.

- Click Next to select or create music to add to your story. There is a wide variety of choices in the Create Music section (eg, classical, rock, film soundtracks suited to various genres).

- Click Next to reach the final step: saving your story in the format that suits your intended purpose for it, such as playing it back on your computer or sending it as an email. Your story will be played in the Windows Media Player format. You may like to burn it onto a CD to share with family and friends.

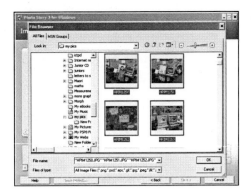

Select and import your photos into Photo Story 3.

In the text menu, you can add text and adjust the font and size.

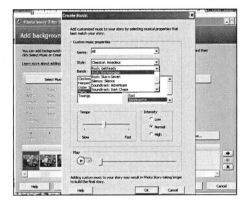

If you decide to add music to your story from the selection available in the Create Music section, you have a wide variety of choices.

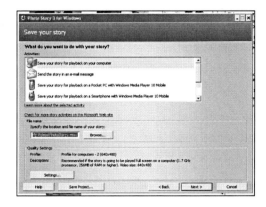

There are a number of options for how you can save your story, based on your intended use for it. Save your story in the Windows Media Player format.

Movie Maker

Windows Movie Maker is a program in the Accessories menu that is bundled with basic PC software. Use it to create movies with still or moving images. To share your video with others, save it to QuickTime Movie or Windows Media Player format.

 For online tutorials on using Windows Movie Maker, see Atomic Learning (movies.atomiclearning.com/k12/moviemaker2) or Georgia Movie Academy (edtech.kennesaw.edu/nisa/moviemaker.htm).

iMovie

iMovie is a video editing program that is bundled with the iLife suite of programs on the Mac. Use it to create videos with still or moving images. To share your video with others, save it to QuickTime Movie or DVD format.

 For online tutorials on using iMovie, see Apple (www.apple.com/ilife/tutorials/#imovie) or School of Information, University of Texas (www.ischool.utexas.edu/technology/tutorials/graphics/imovie/1create.html).

PowerPoint

PowerPoint is a powerful ICT tool that allows you to create slide shows with still photos or videos that include audio and text. It is a dual platform program (ie, available for both Mac and PC), though not all features are available in both operating systems.

The following are some of the key features of PowerPoint:

- Use the **action buttons** and **hyperlink** function to link a page to another page in the PowerPoint slide show, to a document or to a website (see the screenshots that follow).

- With the **custom animation features**, you can create an exciting presentation or slide show by animating letters and objects (see the screenshots that follow).

- Use the **Record Narration** feature (under Slide Show in the top menu bar) to add narration to your slide show.

- Because all the **Word features** are linked to PowerPoint, you can insert tables, charts, pictures, movie clips and more in your PowerPoint slide show.

- Use the Word **drawing tools**, such as WordArt, to create great titles.

Here are some excellent ways to put these features to use:

- Using the action buttons and hyperlink function, make a digital learning centre for the children to click on pictures or words and link to interactive games on websites or special documents (including other slide show presentations). See the final part of this section for more on digital learning centres.

- Insert children's photos in a PowerPoint slide show and ask them to key in their names on the text bar.

- Make alphabet or word–picture slide shows where the letters appear in different ways and, with Record Narration, add timed narration.

- Make animated tangrams so that children can see how to create pictures using shapes.

- Create animated stories where the characters move.

- PowerPoint slide shows are also a great form of presentation with parents and guardians. You can insert videos, photos and charts showing progress and achievement. You can even record children's narrations using Record Narration.

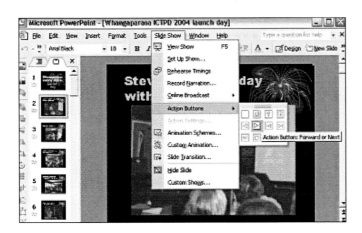

When you select Action Buttons from the Slide Show menu (top menu bar), this browser pops up so you can choose a purpose for your button.

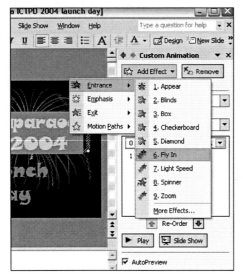

When you select Custom Animation from the Slide Show menu (top menu bar), you can choose from a wide range of effects to animate your text or objects. If the AutoPreview box at the bottom is ticked, your animation will be automatically played for previewing.

You can specify the direction, the speed and the trigger (a mouse click or a set time) for your animation. The pane on the left shows the order in which the animations will appear; the same numbers will be shown in the working form of your PowerPoint file.

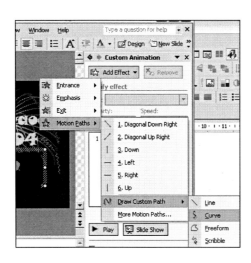

If you have PowerPoint for PC (not Mac), you can create a motion path for your animation and set the motion for any object or text.

For online tutorials on using PowerPoint, see Sonia Coleman's Digital Studio (www.soniacoleman.com/Tutorials/tutorials.htm) or Digital Education Network (www.actden.com).

Using PowerPoint

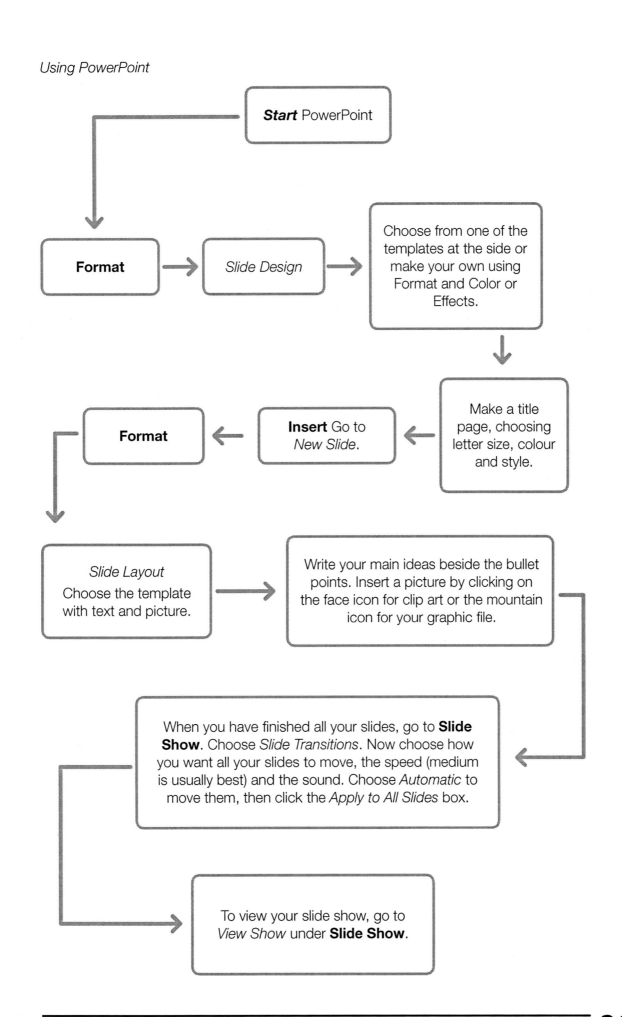

Start PowerPoint

Format → *Slide Design* → Choose from one of the templates at the side or make your own using Format and Color or Effects.

Format ← **Insert** Go to *New Slide*. ← Make a title page, choosing letter size, colour and style.

Slide Layout Choose the template with text and picture. → Write your main ideas beside the bullet points. Insert a picture by clicking on the face icon for clip art or the mountain icon for your graphic file.

When you have finished all your slides, go to **Slide Show**. Choose *Slide Transitions*. Now choose how you want all your slides to move, the speed (medium is usually best) and the sound. Choose *Automatic* to move them, then click the *Apply to All Slides* box.

To view your slide show, go to *View Show* under **Slide Show**.

Podcasting – creating your own radio station on the web

Here's something new to try: following a simple process, you can start your own radio station on the Internet. It's a great way to communicate with family and friends of the children. Each week you could record a new episode on your site.

To begin with, you record the children's stories and experiences on a sound editing program such as GarageBand (Mac) or Audacity (PC). Then you upload the recordings on your own free Internet site. You can make the site secure and password protected so only invited listeners can have access to it. For details, read on …

 Listen to some educational podcasts at the Education Podcast Network (www.epnweb.org).

Recording your podcast with GarageBand

GarageBand comes bundled with the Mac and has an inbuilt microphone. Follow these steps to record your podcast with GarageBand:

- Click on Create a New Podcast.
- On the top menu bar, choose the Track menu and then New Track.
- Choose Real Instrument from the pop-up menu that appears and then choose Vocals (setting to either male or female basic).
- To record, click the red button; to stop, either click the red button again or hit the space bar.
- If you like, add a jingle or some background music to your track. Make sure you have the volume control up for the voice when recording and the volume down for the music so the voice comes through clearly. (Always use the Help menu if you are unsure – that is what it is there for!)
- Go to the Share menu and choose Export to iTunes.
- In iTunes, hold down the Ctrl key and click on the recording and choose Convert to MP3. Alternatively, go to iTunes and choose Preferences, then choose the Advanced tab and Importing; select Import using MP3 or MP4 then, when you export from GarageBand, it will be imported into iTunes as an MP3 or MP4 file, which is the file format needed for loading on to the web.

Recording your podcast with Audacity

Audacity is a free download that can be used for podcast recording with a PC, along with a microphone. Follow these steps to record your podcast with Audacity:

- Plug your microphone into the microphone socket for recording.
- Open Audacity (blue and yellow icon with a headset) and go to Edit Preferences to choose the device (microphone).
- Go to Project on the top menu bar and choose New Audio Track.
- When you are ready to record, press the red button and speak. When you are

finished, press the blue stop button. Press the purple button to get your recording to the beginning and press the green play button to hear your recording.

- When you are happy with your recording, go to File on the top menu bar and choose Export in MP3 format. Export this file to iTunes (which you can download onto a PC if you don't have it).

 Download Audacity for free from SourceForge (www.sourceforge.net).

Creating your own podcasting site

Various sites are available for creating your podcast site. A good place to start is Podomatic:

- Go to the website (www.podomatic.com) and click on the option for creating your own podcast.
- Follow the prompts to create your own username and password and set up the site.
- Click on My Podcast to see what your site looks like, edit your profile or add new posts to the site.
- When you add a post, specify exactly where in iTunes your recording is and state the type of media it has been recorded in (eg, MP3 or MP4). You can put in art work at this stage too.

 To create your own podcast site, go to the Podomatic host site (www.podomatic.com).

When you are setting it up, make sure you do not choose the options to make it public. Instead, give family and friends the link to your site and the password so that they can go there and hear the latest recordings from the children.

Some tips for effective podcasting are to:

- plan well ahead, perhaps using mat time to brainstorm for ideas for the children's podcast
- make podcasts interesting and varied – for example, with interviews, songs, children's stories and poems, and discussion of special events or trips
- give children time to practise first and gain a clear idea of what they are doing.

Some ideas for desktop publishing

There are numerous options open to you for desktop publishing. You can achieve some great results with widely available software, such as Word and PowerPoint. Here are just a few ideas, covering how to:

- set up your workspace so that it is easy to work in
- put your images into shapes with borders
- introduce text
- finetune graphics to prepare them for publication
- make and refine tables.

Setting up your workspace in Word or PowerPoint

Each of the drawing tools in Word and PowerPoint is accessible under the various menus on the top menu bar. When you are working with them frequently, though, it is much easier to have them sitting in a toolbar at the bottom or side of your page:

- To get the toolbars you need up on the screen, go to Toolbars under the View menu in the top menu bar, then tick the toolbars you need.

- To move a toolbar around on the page, click at the end of the toolbar and use the move tool to drag it to the place you want it.

- Hover your cursor over each tool to find out what it does; some tools bring up a menu.

The same wide range of drawing tools is available in both Word and PowerPoint.

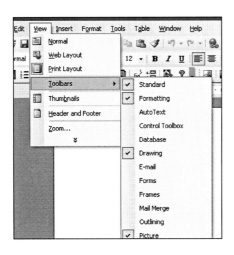

To get the toolbars you need up on the screen, go to Toolbars under the View menu, then tick the toolbars you need.

Put your images into shapes with borders

You can use shapes and borders in Word or PowerPoint to present a photo or another graphic in an eye-catching way:

- Click on AutoShapes in the drawing toolbar to choose your shape. Then click and drag on the page to form your shape. To change the size, drag the white circles that appear around your shape. To rotate the shape, click and drag the green circle that appears on the outside of the shape.

- Click on the arrow beside the fill bucket to get the fill menu. Choose Fill Effects to get the option of adding your own graphic.

- Select your picture and it will fit exactly inside your shape.

- To put a fancy border around your picture, choose Format AutoShape from the Format menu on the top menu bar. Use the Line options to create the effect you want around the shape. (The Fill options apply to your picture inside the shape.) You can also use the 3D tool (available in the drawing toolbar) to create a 3D effect around your shape.

- To put an exciting border around the whole page, choose the Borders and Shading option in the Format menu on the top menu bar.

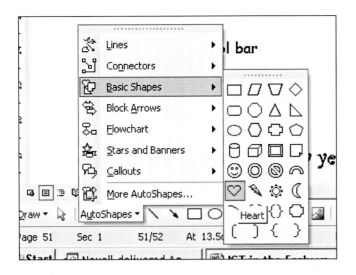

You can put your photos and other images into any shape. Make your children into little stars or hearts!

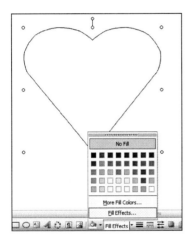

Fill Effects in the fill menu offers you the option of filling your chosen shape with your own graphic.

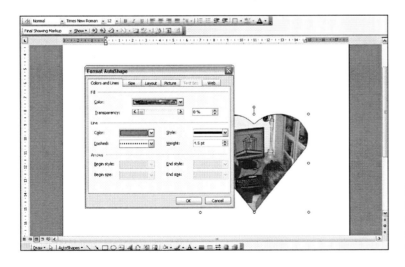

To put a fancy border around your picture, choose Format Autoshape from the Format menu in the top menu bar and choose from the options under Line.

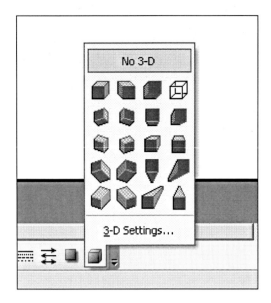

Use the 3D tool in the drawing toolbar to create a 3D effect around your shape.

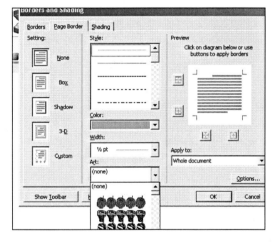

Use the Borders and Shading option in the Format menu on the top of the page. You can create an exciting page border.

Introducing text

Use the text box tool in Word or PowerPoint to create a box where you can key in your text. By moving the text box, you can move your text anywhere on the page. To make a stylish text box (with colour, texture, pattern and/or a border), click on your text box to highlight it and then go to Text Box in the Format menu on the top menu bar.

You can also use callouts (available under the AutoShapes menu), which work in a similar way to text boxes. With them, you can create speech and thought bubbles to accompany your graphics (see example below).

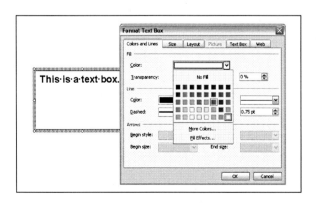

Use a text box to place your text wherever you want it on the page. Under Text Box in the Format menu, there are plenty of options for formatting it too.

This thought bubble is a callout from the AutoShapes menu, which is overlaid on the photo.

Finetuning your graphics

The Picture toolbar in Word and PowerPoint allows you to:

* adjust the contrast and brightness of your graphic
* crop your graphic
* choose how to position your graphic in relation to the text (text wrapping)
* rotate your graphic
* compress your graphic (ie, reduce the file size) for publishing on the web or emailing. (For more on the compressing function, see the information on Publisher under "Working with graphics" above.)

Click on Layout in the Format Picture pop-up box to choose how to position your graphic in relation to the text.

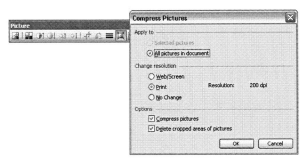

Compressing your graphics is one of many options available from the Picture toolbar of Word and PowerPoint. Use Save As to save the compressed picture with a different name (eg, with "web" added to the end), keeping your original graphic.

Use the Draw menu to:

- layer your graphics (with the Order command)

- position your graphics in the same alignment with one another or so that they are evenly distributed across the page (Align or Distribute)

- change a graphic's orientation (Rotate or Flip)

- alter the shape of a graphic, if you have created it with an AutoShape (Change AutoShape).

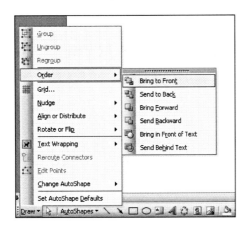

The range of options available from the Draw menu includes options for layering your graphics. Bring to Front, for example, will mean the selected graphic appears in the top layer, in front of all other graphics.

Making a table

It is easy to make a table and finetune it in Word or PowerPoint:

- Create a table by choosing the Insert option from the Table menu on the top menu bar or by clicking on the table icon on the Tables and Borders toolbar. In the pop-up menu that appears, specify how many rows or columns you want in your table (though you can always change your mind later and insert or delete any number of rows or columns).

- If you wish to add a heading in the top row of the table, select all the cells in the top row and choose the Merge Cells option from the Table menu on the top toolbar (or right-click in the selected cells and choose from the pop-up menu that appears.)

- Alternatively, to split a single cell in half, select the relevant cell and choose Split Cells from the Table menu.

- To finetune your table, go to Table Properties in the Table menu. Here you can determine features such as the alignment of the table on the page, the alignment of text within each cell and the size of each row and column. With the Borders and Shading option, you can also specify the appearance of the lines within and around the table.

- As a shortcut to altering the size of any column or row, hover over the relevant table line until you see the line with double arrows, then click and drag the line to increase or decrease your column or row.

46

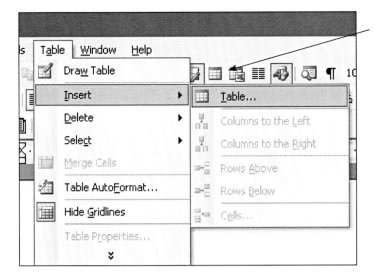

Clicking the table icon is an alternative way to make a table.

To create a table, go to the Table menu on the top menu bar, then choose Insert and finally Table. In the pop-up menu that appears, you can specify the number of rows and columns for your table.

To join together all the cells in a single row (eg, to create a heading), scroll across to select all the cells in the row and choose Merge Cells from the Table menu on the top menu bar.

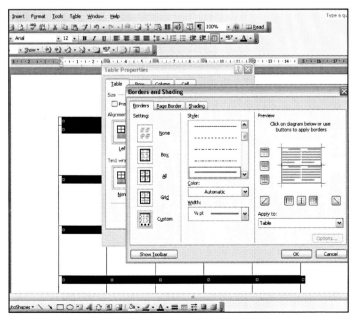

The Borders and Shading function is accessible from Table Properties under the Table menu. Here you can create or remove grid lines within and around the table, and change their thickness, style and colour.

47

Creating learning stories

One of the most successful ways of enhancing learning with the variety of digital learning tools available is to implement learning stories. ICT tools enhance the learning stories by providing a medium for recording still and moving images and by providing a medium for sharing the stories with a wider audience.

What are learning stories?

The concept of learning stories in the early childhood sector came from the seminal work by Dr Margaret Carr. Her project for the Assessment for Learning exemplars forms the basis for assessment in the early childhood sector.

Learning stories are a form of narrative assessment. Significant learning episodes are recorded in the form of a story about learning – a personal record that the child can look at and reflect on. With guided conversation between teacher and child, the next steps in learning can be discussed and the story forms a basis for sharing learning experiences with others, notably family members. These stories may be reciprocal in that family members may document learning experiences at home as well. The learning stories are gathered together in an individual child's portfolio and chart the progress of the child's learning in an authentic and relevant way.

The following software is helpful in creating learning stories:

- Word documents or KidPix or PowerPoint slide shows – to display photos and add text, which may be taken from the children who look at the photos and dictate the text
- PowerPoint or Photo Story 3 – to add narration, which children themselves can provide through a recording of their spoken story
- a video editing program, such as Movie Maker or iMovie – to edit footage.

Useful hardware to support the creation of these learning stories includes:

- the digital still camera – to provide immediate viewing feedback
- the digital video camera – to record significant learning events as they happen
- a TV, a data projector and screen, or an interactive whiteboard – to share videos with others.

C. Case studies

This section outlines what some early childhood centres are doing with ICT tools to enhance learning.

Unitec Early Childhood Centre

At the Unitec Early Childhood Centre in Auckland, New Zealand, the teachers and children use the digital still and video cameras to record learning experiences. They view them on the special widescreen TV and also share interactive learning CD-ROM activities on the laptop and stationary computer in the centre. Plans are in progress to purchase a data projector and screen so the electronic data can be shared with a wider audience.

Janice, the centre supervisor, talked about a successful ICT learning experience stemming from the theme of dinosaurs. Teachers photographed the centre's small plastic dinosaurs, cropped the photos in Photoshop, and then superimposed the dinosaur photos over existing photos in distant locations. Each day they showed a different dinosaur in a different location around the world. With their parents and guardians, the children dictated letters to the dinosaurs, which were emailed or taken in hard copy form from their home to the centre. As well as involving the parents, this approach helped the children to learn about other parts of the world in a meaningful way through visual imagery and discussion with teachers and family.

Another recent successful ICT learning experience was the digital recording of the children making up recipes. The recording was made into a PowerPoint slide show, which was used for discussion about the processes involved in cooking.

Children at the Unitec Early Childhood Centre use Begin to Learn to classify and group concepts.

Kiwi Care Preschool

Kiwi Care Preschool in Auckland, New Zealand employs only fully qualified staff (ie, those with an early childhood education diploma). Staff member and ICT coordinator Liz and supervisor Rachel work together to enable all children to have access to and learn about ICT tools.

The centre's Activboard (Promethean interactive whiteboard: see Section A) is constantly used by the children and staff in a variety of ways. Children view videos about themselves, which are often used as a reflective tool for learning. Each month the centre holds a concert and the children view their own practices so they can see where they may make improvements or changes to their performance.

Videos displayed on the interactive whiteboard are also used as a reflective tool about play; often children see themselves in the act of learning, review their learning experiences and discuss their learning experiences with others. For example, one little girl observed herself pushing a boy away from the dance session she was having with another group of girls. When she viewed the video, she could see the look of hurt on his face as he walked away and was excluded from their play. By realising what she had done and what the effect was on the other person, she could think through her actions and their effects on others.

Taking videos and photos is an everyday happening at this centre. Children know how to load the pictures on to the computer and are experts in using the computer, even being able to display it on the interactive whiteboard during mat time. Often the children take the mat time sessions with teacher supervision. They have a folder and can choose their own favourite websites with activities they interact with on the Activboard. One of their favourite activities is to "Google the world", exploring the world through the satellite imagery and range of geographical information available at Google Earth. They also have their own flipcharts (Activboard folder) where they store their own work. One of the advantages of using this interactive whiteboard is that the screen is huge and set at the children's height so they can interact more readily with the content.

 To Google the world, visit Google Earth (earth.google.com).

Children take charge of the camera at Kiwi Care Preschool.

Liz, who is a graduate of the Unitec Early Childhood Diploma, is a firm believer in using the correct terminology with the children. Guided by this working principle, the children are developing an understanding of the features and concepts involved in the use of the digital camera, computer and Activboard.

Liz has also taught some of the older children how to: centre the image on a camera and focus; use the different modes on the camera such as still or video image; use the webcam; change the batteries; and load pictures on to the computer.

These children love to help others to learn and so the use of ICT tools becomes a natural progression with peer tutoring.

The children open their images in Paint and draw and write on them. They know how to zoom in and paint in detail over their pictures. They understand about using a full screen mode and many other concepts that will transfer to other areas of knowledge in the world of ICT tools.

As well as recently sharing their knowledge at the ULearn Information and Communications Technology Professional Development (ICTPD) national conference, Liz and Rachel regularly share their knowledge at staff meetings. There is also a special time for staff to engage in professional development to learn about ICT skills so that all the staff can engage in the integration of ICT tools into the centre.

One of the special features of the centre is its concerts performed by the children. The centre staff make videos of the concerts and other events or trips and one staff member edits them, using Pinnacle Studio, to create DVDs to share. The centre then sells the DVDs for a nominal price. In this way, families can share in the happenings at the centre even when they are not able to attend due to work commitments. The children are also able to revisit their experiences on the Activboard.

ICT tools are integrated into the everyday learning at Kiwi Care Preschool. Children are empowered to be confident users of the tools.

D. Internet sites for the early years

These website addresses (URLs) are correct at the time of publication. If you have trouble accessing any of them, it may help to undertake an Internet search for them using the additional information on the left.

Educational games and activities

Author and/or name of site	URL
Julie Tonnu et al, JayZeeBear	www.jayzeebear.com/bird_house.html *Selection of interactive games (suitable for interactive whiteboard or using at the computer)*
Roxie Carroll, A Kids Heart	www.akidsheart.com/threer/lvl1/shapes.htm *Interactive games*
Jerry Jindrich, Sorting Fish	www.meddybemps.com/deepblue/sortingfish.html *Interactive activity*
JigZone, Jigsaw Puzzle Paradise	www.jigzone.com *Make your own jigsaws and even use your own photos (free, but you need to join)*
Welcome to Bry-Back Manor	www.bry-backmanor.org *Interactive activities for the Mac, plus printable items for Mac or PC*
BBC, CBeebies	www.bbc.co.uk/cbeebies/somethingspecial/games *A really good site with interactive games and activities – suitable for interactive whiteboard too*
Sesame Workshop, Sesame Street	www.sesameworkshop.org/sesamestreet *Fun interactive games and activities*
Topmarks, Primary Interactive Whiteboard Resources	www.topmarks.co.uk/Interactive.aspx *Interactive maths games – suitable for the interactive whiteboard too*
Fisher Price, Catch-a-Crazy Daisy Game	www.fisher-price.com/us/fun/games/crazydaisy/#game *Interactive games for various levels*
Jerry Jindrich, Tippety Witchet's Magic Paint Brush	www.meddybemps.com/MagicPaint.html *Use like Paint to create pictures – potentially a good activity on the interactive whiteboard*
Planet Interactive, Learning Planet Preschool/Kindergarten Activities	www.learningplanet.com/parents1.htm *Interactive games to develop numeracy and literacy*
Jenny Eather, Rainforest Maths	www.rainforestmaths.com *Interactive maths activities for primary levels*

Educational games and activities (continued)

Author and/or name of site	URL
Literacy Web at the University of Connecticut, Preschool Webquests	www.literacy.uconn.edu/pkwebqu.htm *Simple WebQuests on animals, community helpers and rhymes*
KidsPlayPark	www.kidsplaypark.com/games *Maths, art, memory and word games*
Ma Hubbard's Create-a-Reader	www.create-a-reader.com *Interactive educational games on literacy and numeracy – suitable for interactive whiteboard*

Music and stories

Author and/or name of site	URL
Educators' Circle, Songs for Teaching: Using Music to Promote Learning	www.songsforteaching.com *Listen and sing along to numerous songs*
Lil' Fingers, Storybooks	www.lil-fingers.com/storybooks *Really good site for electronic stories*
Carol Moore, Children's Storybooks Online	www.magickeys.com/books *A range of electronic stories*
Public Library of Charlotte and Mecklenburg County, StoryPlace Pre-school Library	www.storyplace.org/preschool/other.asp *Electronic stories categorised by theme and accompanied by various activities*
Goodnight Stories	www.goodnightstories.com/stories.htm *Electronic stories in various formats (eg, for reading, listening to, filling in)*
Starfall Education, Learn to Read at Starfall	www.starfall.com *Literacy activities for beginners*

Templates and other resources

Author and/or name of site	URL
Preschool Education, Preschool Printables	www.preschoolprintables.com *Printable certificates and other items*
Elizabeth Bushey, Inkless Tales	www.inklesstales.com/alphabet/k.shtml *Animated alphabet*
abcteach	abcteach.com *Mainly printable resources*
Pure Clipart	www.pureclipart.com *A huge range of categorised clip art, free for non-commercial use*

References

Clarke, S, Timperley, H and Hattie, J (2004) *Unlocking Formative Assessment.* NZ ed. Auckland: Hodder Moa Beckett.

Ministry of Education (1996) *Te Whariki: He Whariki Matauranga mo nga Mokopuna o Aotearoa: Early Childhood Curriculum.* Wellington: Ministry of Education.

Ministry of Education (2006a) *Foundations for Discovery.* Retrieved from www.minedu. govt.nz, 20 November 2006.

Ministry of Education (2006b) *The New Zealand Curriculum: Draft for consultation.* Wellington: Learning Media.

Index of ICT tools